12 Rules Of Being A Powerful Woman

SARAH ORDO

FOREWORD BY CARA ALWILL LEYBA

12 Rules Of Being A Powerful Woman

ISBN: 9781690009351

Foreword

Have you ever found yourself sitting in a conference room at work, surrounded by men in positions of power, terrified to raise your hand? Or maybe you've been in a relationship with someone who takes every opportunity to make you feel stupid when you talk about your big dreams. Perhaps you've been laughed at by a group of "mean girls" – or perhaps, you've been disempowered by the biggest bully of all – yourself.

In those moments, we have two choices. We can remain silent, small, and fearful, or we can lean into the biggest, boldest, most brilliant version of ourselves. We can lean into our power.

It's not easy to be a woman, but I wouldn't trade it for the world. In fact, I'm damn proud of us. We've had to fight for our place in society and we're not done yet. We continue to rise up, make waves, elevate each other, and teach the next generation of women to be even better. We're raising babies and businesses and banishing the limiting beliefs that have been ingrained in us for so long. We have an incredible inner strength, and an immeasurable amount of potential available to us in any moment of any day to do anything we set our minds to.

But how exactly do we tap that potential? How do we move through the social conditioning that has told us to sit down and be quiet for so long? How do we raise our hand, brush off that mean girl, or look that lover in the face and tell him, "I'm doing it anyway"? How do we finally and completely love ourselves enough to become our own best friend and build a life we're proud of?

In this book, Sarah Ordo will show you how. She will walk you through twelve powerful mindset shifts that will challenge your fears and help you realize that you had the power all along.

Sarah walks her walk. She's not just writing this book – she's living it. Every day, with every ounce of her own personal strength. You'll learn more about Sarah's journey through these pages, but as someone who has had the privilege of watching her rise up from her own ashes and dedicate her life to empowering women around the world, I can genuinely say that you'll be learning these rules from a pro.

I encourage you to soak these words up. Allow them to fill you with the hope you may have misplaced. Let this book guide you toward your best, most powerful self – the woman who has been waiting for you to come home to her.

She's ready.

Hey Ladies!

The women of today have started a movement.

Women today are making moves, taking risks, and rewriting the damn thing in every way possible! We are starting successful businesses, organizing marches, paying our own bills, proudly sharing our stories, raising children on our own, speaking up, and changing how women will be seen forever.

It is such an inspiring, empowering time to be a woman!

Being a woman, a female entrepreneur, a voice, and a writer in the online space, I felt like this book was one that I was long overdue to self-publish.

(That's right...SELF-PUBLISH. Because I am one of those POWERFUL f***ing women who took things into my own hands and made my dreams a reality. WOO!)

This book has been made for all of you women out there, by a woman that sees and knows the power you have within you. She had to find that power within herself first. But, when she did...MAGIC started to happen. Now, it's your turn to find yours.

This book was made with so much love, passion, and heart that I know it will connect with you and ignite a fire deep inside of your own heart. To boost your confidence. To give yourself permission. To realize how strong you are. To realize how beautiful you are. To become the powerful woman you were ALWAYS meant to be.

Powerful women are taking over the game, and I am BEYOND honored to be a part of this movement with you.

xoxo,
Sarah

1. She Will Not Be Silenced

WE REALIZE THE
IMPORTANCE OF OUR
VOICES ONLY WHEN WE
ARE SILENCED.

-Malala
Yousafzai

She Will Not Be Silenced

We've all done it. We've sat quiet while things happened in our lives that didn't feel good. We've allowed someone else to speak for us because we didn't feel confident enough to speak up for ourselves.

We've allowed others to talk over us and louder than us because we didn't feel what we had to say was as big, as impactful or as important as their words were. We've stayed silent when what we really wanted to do was speak.

Well, girl...F*** that noise.

Forget what you were taught. Forget what you were told. Forget whatever you might have convinced yourself. Stop thinking that your voice doesn't matter. Drop the idea that what you have to say is any less valuable or relevant than what anyone else is saying.

**We were given a voice for one reason.
To use it.**

When I was younger, I was a painfully shy little girl. I was taught to be ladylike, to stay in my lane, to not be too loud, and to do what was expected of me. ALWAYS.

I attended a private Catholic School where you weren't allowed to wear bright nail polish, speak without raising your hand for permission first, and God forbid you roll your plaid uniform skirt to hit above that knee! *Gasp*

**I stayed inside the lines and stayed quiet.
Real quiet.**

In my school, you walked in straight lines down the hallway with a finger over your lips to keep yourself quiet. You silenced yourself because those were the rules you had been taught. You held your own finger over your lips and made sure that you stayed quiet.

We were taught from a very young age to be silent, to not speak out of turn, and to be disciplined enough to keep ourselves that way.

Let's just say that when I started public school it was like an episode of f***ing Breaking Amish. I wanted to test the waters and get loud. They always say that its the quiet ones you need to look out for, and boy, did they hit the nail on the head with that one!

I broke out of that cookie cutter mold, alright. For the first time in my life I didn't need to walk down a hallway with a finger held over my lips.

I was free to do what I wanted, Be who I wanted, And get as loud as I wanted.

How many of us grew up as women that were told to walk in that straight line with that finger held over their lips? How many of us feel like we've still been told to do it sometimes as a grown a** woman?

How many of you reading this have felt like you had to bite your tongue in life when you really wanted to be screaming from the rooftops?

How many of us have sat quiet when we had something to say? Something important. Something that mattered to us. Something that stirred in our hearts. Something powerful. Something that could change the world.

Discovering your voice is such an empowering and transformative experience in life as a woman. Harnessing the power you have in your words is a big move. Deciding that you will not be silenced is an even bigger one.

Being a powerful woman means using your voice.

It means refusing to sit down and be quiet when you have something on your heart. It means defying the past idea that we shouldn't speak up. That takes strength. That takes courage. That takes confidence.

Women have fought for us to have this freedom and opportunity to use our voice, and it is an absolute shame when we choose to not take that right and use it.

Stand up. Speak up. Get loud. Use your voice. Speak your truth.

But, most importantly, make sure that you are using it for good. Make sure that the things you communicate are promoting equality, love, acceptance, and inspiration. Use your voice to lift others up and to change the world.

One voice can make an impact. One voice can change everything. Why can't it be yours?

You never know how much your words can change the world. You never know how much your voice can impact the lives of others. You never know how many women you can inspire to stand up, to not be silenced, and to start using their own voices.

Being a powerful woman is all about the way you choose to live every single day. Never allowing yourself to be silenced, quieted, or told that what you have to say doesn't matter.

You are a powerful woman

2. She Loves Herself First & Fearlessly

YOUR TASK IS NOT TO
SEEK FOR LOVE, BUT
MERELY TO SEEK AND
FIND ALL THE BARRIERS
WITHIN YOURSELF THAT
YOU HAVE BUILT
AGAINST IT.

-Rumi

She Loves Herself First
& Fearlessly

We see self love posted EVERYWHERE nowadays. It's hashtagged on your favorite Instagram model's post while she takes a bubble bath. It's talked about on personal development podcasts everywhere you turn. It's also your best girlfriend's favorite justification everytime she buys herself another expensive pair of heels.

Self love goes way deeper than just buying yourself the shoes.

Loving ourselves first and foremost may seem selfish to some women, especially if it is a new concept to them. This is because traditionally we are taught that women are nurtures, caregivers, and mothers. We are wired to think that we innately should look at others and ask them what they need first.

We often look outward to give our love away to others before we look inward and ask if we need it ourselves.

Look inward first.

It might feel wierd. It might feel narcissistic. It might feel like you are the most vapid, self-centered person in the world. But, guess what? To a certain extent, you need to be that way.

It shouldn't feel wrong to love yourself.

I first explored the love I had for myself when I got sober. For the first time in my life I didn't have alcohol to lean on, and it stripped back ALL the layers. It forced me to look at how I was living my life. It also forced me to face the f***ed up relationship I had with myself for years.

I didn't love myself first. I barely loved myself at all.

When I realized how freely I gave my love away and how little I gave it to myself, it was mind-boggling and pretty sad. So, I started intentionally figuring out how to love myself. At first, it felt like riding a bicycle for the first time without training wheels...awkward and f***ing uncomfortable.

I always thought that I loved myself.

I mean, I bought myself nice things, I felt confident, and I always posted all of those Pinterest quotes about self love all over my social media. But, I soon realized that self love isn't just about those things.

It is so much deeper than that.

Loving yourself is about acceptance. It is about being at peace with yourself on the inside. Sometimes its about easy things like treating yourself to a face mask before bed. Sometimes it is about bigger heavier things like choosing to leave a toxic relationship or ending the negative self talk towards yourself. It is about asking what YOU need...and then giving yourself whatever that is over and over and over again.

Self love is a journey.

It might not happen overnight and you might need to work really f***ing hard at it. It's time to get to work. Girl, it's LONG overdue.

Dive into the things that you love about yourself. Figure out what makes you unique. Figure out what makes you a one of a kind woman. Eliminate the judgement. Stop telling yourself that you are not enough. You are enough.

You have ALWAYS been enough.

We all go through seasons and stages of life where things are difficult and things aren't perfect. There's times when things don't make sense and there's times when we don't feel our best. What's crucial is that we learn how to navigate these thoughts, feelings, and situations. To always end up in a place of love.

Love yourself.. And do it fearlessly.

What is there to fear about prioritizing yourself? What could possibly be enough to hold you back from doing it? What reservations do you hold about yourself that keep you from feeling that authentic, unwavering, and relentless love and admiration for the woman that you are?

You are the only one that can make self love happen.

It doesn't matter what anyone in your life says or does. They can't do the work for you. Nobody on the outside can make this one happen for you. This one is on you and only you, baby girl.

Mastering how to love yourself will unlock a whole new woman. That woman is vivacious. She is beautiful. She is strong. She is confident. She is full of life. She is everything a woman should be, and not one thing less.

A powerful woman loves herself first. A powerful woman loves herself fearlessly.

A powerful woman decides that she is enough no matter what anyone else tells her. She's got this. She's always did. She always will. And she's gonna love herself every step of the way.

You are a powerful woman

3. She Does Not Allow Disrespect

RESPECT IS ONE OF
LIFE'S GREATEST
TREASURES. I MEAN,
WHAT DOES IT ALL
ADD UP TO IF YOU
DON'T HAVE THAT?

-Marilyn Monroe

She Does Not Allow Disrespect

Think back on a time that someone made you feel low. Think of a time you let someone say something about you that was degrading. Think about a time that something so out of line happened to you that negativity came hurling at you like a slap in the face. Think about a time when you didn't have the ladyballs to stand up, speak up, and demand that R-E-S-P-E-C-T.

Grow the lady balls. A big ol' pair of 'em.

You'll see some common themes that tie into a lot of the rules in this book, and not standing up for ourselves, who we are, and what we stand for is one of them. This ties directly in to demanding respect as a woman. Not only demanding it, but making sure that you get it.

This means that we know how we deserve to be spoken to, spoken about, and treated by those that we allow into our lives.

Respect should be the norm.

Unfortunately, for a lot of people out there in the world, that's not always the case. This is because we haven't been demanding it and because we've also let a lot of s*** slide over the years. We've made respect into something that is optional and not a requirement.

Not all women in the world will feel like respect is a non-negotiable, and some of them will never see it that way. There are cultural beliefs, personal beliefs, and many other things that play into this. Odds are, if you bought this book you are not one of those women. So, let's get back to the good stuff.

Respect is a requirement, not an option.

What's important is to realize that being respected is the standard we will design our lives by as powerful women. Whether it is as a mother, a caregiver, an entrepreneur, a friend, a mentor, a daughter, a wife, a girlfriend, or any other role we might take on.

I used to allow disrespect in many ways.

Whether it was the respect I wasn't showing myself as a woman, or the respect I wasn't requiring from others, I used to struggle a lot with this one. It took a long time to rewrite the script I had written about respect, but I rewrote the f*** out of it.

I realized that I, too, deserved the respect that I gave to others. I learned that it wasn't okay to be disrespected or shamed by a man for any reason. I learned that I could say, "NO, thats not okay" when something a woman did or said towards me didn't feel right.

You don't ask for it. You demand it.

At some point, my mindset switched over to this new idea. The idea was that we, as women, shouldn't be asking for respect like it's up to someone else to decide whether we receive it or not.

We don't give away that kind of power. We demand respect. We don't make it optional. We make it non-negotiable.

Now, obviously, you can't force someone to be respectful. There will be people that won't receive your message and won't allign with your beliefs. There will be pushback. There will be resistance. There will be opposition.

People might get uncomfortable.

But, guess what? It's not your job to make sure that other people are comfortable with your power and what you want as a woman. It's your job to take your stance and decide what you want your life to look like, feel like, and sound like. Then you design it to reflect that.

Commanding respect does NOT make you a b**.**

It makes you strong, secure, and in tune with how you want to be treated. It gives you a standard for relationships. It ensures that you are given credit for the work that you do. It makes you receive acknowledgement for who you are as a person. There is nothing about demanding those things that is negative, shameful, or wrong.

No matter how insignificant or small it may be, we will not allow it. No little comments will go unaddressed. No sexualization for your appearance will go unacknowledged. No minimizing of your talents and skills will happen without objection.

**It's not okay. It was never okay.
It will never be okay.**

If you haven't started yet, today is the day that you will rewrite the script for how you will be respected as a woman.

It might be uncomfortable. It might challenge everything you've been taught. It might cause life-changing things to happen and shake up the life you've always known and been comfortable living.

Get uncomfortable. Speak up for yourself. Demand the respect you deserve - and have ALWAYS deserved - as a woman.

You are a powerful woman

4. She Follows Her Heart

(With Her Head Close Behind)

YOU CAN DO ANYTHING
AS LONG AS YOU DON'T
STOP BELIEVING. WHEN
IT IS MEANT TO BE, IT
WILL BE. YOU JUST
HAVE TO FOLLOW YOUR
HEART.

-Keke Palmer

She Follows Her Heart
(With Her Head Close Behind)

You know that feeling you get when something is stirring in your heart? That undeniable excitement, passion, and intrigue for something that you simply cannot deny. It might be a big life change, a new significant other, an alternate career path, or a million other things. Your heart just pulls you towards whatever it is.

Your heart sometimes speaks the loudest.

When we were little girls, we did whatever our hearts desired. We had the crush on the boy. We voiced our desire to be ballerinas or female astronauts loud and proud. We wore flourescent hot pink spandex shorts and didn't give a s*** what anyone thought about it.

Ladies, where did those little girls go!?

When did we stop following our hearts...and WHY!? What changed in us that made us stop living out every single one of our deepest desires?

Growing up happened.

Life, responsibilities, children, and paying bills happened. Now, my head isn't too far up in the clouds. I realize that sometimes we cannot simply make our life choices like we did when we were young. I, too, have bills to pay, responsibilities to live up to, and a career to run...I get it.

We cannot throw everything to the wind and live carefree one hundred percent of the time. But, what if we could find some kind of balance? A life where we could follow our heart but also be smart and intentional about it. Have you ever wondered if that was possible?

Girl, it's more than possible.

I believe that a powerful woman can follow her heart, chase after her passions, and live in the moment. But, the thing that is different about the way she does it is that her head is close behind. Confused? Allow me to elaborate.

Following your heart and your innermost desires can be risky. It can be careless. It can get you into a financial mess. It can ruin your relationships. It can make some people in your life think that you've absolutely lost it. This is where the balance part comes in.

A powerful woman knows that she can follow her heart, but she is also responsible about it. She makes life choices based on passion, desires, and dreams, but she also considers how to do it in a way that is smart and not reckless.

You can absolutely follow your heart and use your head at the same time.

A powerful woman jumps, but she makes sure she has a little bit of a landing zone prepared just in case. She falls in love, but doesn't get blinded to the reality of who someone else really is. She makes big career moves, but doesn't leave herself broke and unable to survive.

She thinks of the bigger picture, not just the immediate one.

When I decided to leave my college degree in the dust, start my own business, and be self-employed, I did it smart. I chased after my dreams relentlessly! I spent every single day building my business. But, I also made sure that I wasn't going to get myself into a mess along the way.

I knew that I would be successful. I knew that I would make it. I was so passionate about what was in my heart that there was no way I wouldn't make it work. But I was always logical about it along the way. My heart led the journey, but never completely on her own.

I kept my head shotgun for the ride.

I say all of this to not damper the fire that burns in yout heart to achieve big things. I'm not trying to hold you back or tell you to play small. I'm telling you to run after what your heart tells you to run after! But also use your head while you are on your way.

Balance, girl. BALANCE.

A powerful woman knows she is capable of everything and anything she sets her mind to. She knows that she can follow her heart in every move she makes in her life. And she knows she can do it in a way that is intentional, smart, and on purpose.

A powerful woman chases after the life of her dreams.

She knows that she can have the life she dreams of. She knows she can chase after every crazy dream she has. She can have everything her heart desires and MORE.

She knows she can have it all.

And she knows that she can do it in a way that is daring and brave, yet grounded and pragmatic. This is what makes her so powerful. The understanding that she can follow her heart while also keeping her head close behind.

You are a powerful woman

5. She Has Her Own Opinions & Beliefs

I HAVE LEARNED THAT
AS LONG AS I HOLD
FAST TO MY BELIEFS
AND VALUES - AND
FOLLOW MY OWN MORAL
COMPASS - THEN THE
ONLY EXPECTATIONS I
NEED TO LIVE UP TO
ARE MY OWN.

-Michelle Obama

She Has Her Own Opinions & Beliefs

Now, I'm about to quote a man for this one. Yes, I know, this is a book all about empowering women, but there are lots of extremely intelligent men we can learn a lot from out there in the world! Alexander Hamilton once said, "If you don't stand for something, you will fall for anything."

The man had a point...a damn good one.

We have the right to stand up for certain beliefs, opinions, and morals that we have as women. Not only as women, but as human beings. If you don't take advantage of that right, you'll just follow someone else and what they believe in instead.

We didn't always have these rights.

Even though it seems unimaginable in today's society, there was a time where you wouldn't be able to stand up and voice that opinion.

We've come a long, long way.

I can't imagine a world where I would be told to sit down, be quiet, and not be listened to as an adult woman. I can't fathom a world where I didn't get to vote on important issues and who would lead my country. As hard as it is for me to imagine it, I know that was the way things were in the past.

We, as women, were given rights to use them.

We were given the right to vote. We were given the right to run for political positions. We were given the right to have the same job titles as men. And we also got to a point where the color of our skin, our religious beliefs, and our sexual orientation no longer prohibits us from what we chose to do in life.

Now, we aren't perfect with it as a society just yet. But I think we can all agree that we have a lot more freedom, more rights, and a lot more people listening to the opinions and beliefs of women today than we ever have at any other point in history.

A powerful woman owns her opinion.

We are free to decide what opinion we have about any person, place, or thing in life. We have the right to decide that we don't like something. We have the freedom to decide who we want to be a part of our lives. We have the freedom to say "NO" to things that don't feel right.

Your beliefs don't have to match anyone else's.

That's the beauty of beliefs. We, as women, can have any belief that we feel is a reflection of ourselves and what we align with. Whether it be religious, political, or personal...they are ours. This means that they are valid. They are valuable. They are real.

Another important thing is to realize that not everyone will agree with your opinions and beliefs. Some people will have opposing opinions. Some people won't passionately believe the same things you do. And that's absolutely okay.

People can disagree with what you believe.

And they absolutely will! Some of them wont be quiet about it either. Some of them might even be disrespectful and rude about it. I mean, have ya'll checked the comments section on anything viral on social media lately? People love to show up and stir things up!

Just as I'm getting all fired up preaching about having our own beliefs, I've got to hold all of you accountable for the other side of things as well. If you are going to have your own opinions and beliefs and stand proud with them, you've got to allow others to do the same.

It's only right to return the favor.

Let other people have and share their opinions just as you do yours. You can say you don't agree with them, but you dont need to criticize them, attack them, or tear them down for having their own way of thinking about something.

We're better than that, ladies.

A powerful woman does not stoop to that level or take that road. She gives the same level of respect to others as she wishes to receive herself. She practices what she preaches, day in and day out.

She walks the walks and she talks the talk.

As a powerful woman, you should know and live by this rule. Take advantage of the rights we have today. Have your own opinions. Have your own beliefs. You should feel solid and secure in what they are and you should feel free to express them proudly.

Powerful women do not sit quietly and conform to what others think, feel, and believe. They form their own ideas, opinions, and beliefs on things that are important and impactful in their lives. And they are hella passionate about them.

You are a powerful woman

6. She Accepts Every Inch Of Her Physical Self

FEELING BEAUTIFUL HAS
NOTHING TO DO WITH
WHAT YOU LOOK LIKE. I
PROMISE.

-Emma Watson

She Accepts Every Inch Of Her Physical Self

Now this...this one is a big one. This one breaks my heart over and over again when I see it not happening. This is one rule that I have become so aggressively passionate about following in my own life. Mainly because for a long time, I wasn't following it myself.

We are so damn hard on ourselves when it comes to our appearance. We look at models enviously online and in magazines. We look at other women and wish we had their boobs, their hair, their lips. We criticize ourselves for not looking like the women we view as "perfect."

Newsflash: Perfect doesn't exist.

The idea of a "perfect" woman is absolute bull****. There is no textbook standard for what makes a woman "perfect," and there never will be. So drop that idea like it's hot, girl.

We are all beautiful.

What makes us unique and what makes us different is what makes us beautiful. The freckles on our cheeks, the shape of our hips, the color of our skin...all different, all unique, and all truly beautiful in their own way.

This one can go wrong at a very young age.

I remember the first time I did not love every inch of myself. It was in a leotard and tights surrounded by a dozen other girls in my ballet class. My body didn't look like theirs. I didn't have the body of a tall, slender dancer. I was a pre-teen that loved pizza, burgers, and pasta. I was also pushing 4'11" and not hitting a growth spurt anytime soon.

A lot of us, as women, attain an unrealistic idea of what "beautiful" is in our younger years. We convince ourselves that we need to be tall, skinny, and perfectly styled at all times. We correlate our self-confidence and self worth with our physical appearance.

It's a dangerous, slippery slope we start out on.

When I fell into the dangerous trap of connecting my self worth to my physical appearance with an invisible string, I watched myself plummet. It led to myself sitting on the bathroom floor trying to throw up my pizza as a pre-teen. It led to years of having barely any self worth. It led to my thinking that I was only worthy when I looked "perfect" on the outside.

I can guarantee that many of us (including myself) went through a stage in life where we wouldn't leave the house without makeup on. We had to at least put on some foundation and mascara to run to the store. Think about how warped that idea is though in reality...

What do we feel the need to hide?

Why do we feel like we need to hide our natural and beautiful selves? Why does letting someone see who we really are have to be such a bad thing? Where did we get it all so wrong?

Confidence is a very powerful thing.

There is power in being confident in every inch of our physical selves. There is power in owning our jean size, our cellulite, our freckles, and our small bra size. There is power in wearing your wrinkles, dark spots, and stretch marks like a badge of honor. It is pure, un-f***ing-touchable confidence and beauty.

A powerful woman holds her head high knowing that she is beautiful...every single inch of her. She knows that her beauty does not define her, but that she defines her own individual beauty.

She knows that her physical appearance is not what will lead her to find true happiness, success, and love. She knows those things don't come from being "perfect" or fitting a mold of what someone else deems as beautiful.

Those things come from acceptance and love.

A powerful woman loves, accepts, and embraces every part of herself. She does not criticize the body that allows her to move. She does not obsess over the number on the scale. She does not attack the things about her appearance that look different than someone else's.

A powerful woman accepts every single inch of her beautiful self.

She knows the power of confidence. She knows the power of how she carries herself. She knows that by loving every inch of herself, she can (and will) inspire other women to do the same. Now THAT'S beautiful.

A powerful woman looks at herself in the mirror, blows herself a kiss, slaps her own a**, and flips her hair back as she struts out the door. Nobody can stop a woman that owns, loves, and accepts every inch of herself. That type of confidence cannot be broken or stopped. Watch the f*** out world.

You are a powerful woman

1. She Has Big Goals & Even Bigger Dreams

HOW MANY SUCCESS
STORIES DO YOU NEED
TO READ UNTIL YOU
GIVE YOURSELF
PERMISSION TO WRITE
YOUR OWN?

-Kylie Francis

She Has Big Goals & Even Bigger Dreams

Think of the women you look up to. Think of the women that inspire you. Think of the women that you look at and think, "Damn, she's killing it." These women can be your family, your friends, or even people you follow on the internet. You admire the passion in their hearts, their accomplishments, their drive, etc.

These women know they can do big things.

Have you ever caught yourself in a daydream where you picture yourself doing something BIG, something CRAZY, something you doubt you could ever accomplish? Have you ever pictured yourself giving a keynote speech? Starting and running a successful business? Making a difference in the world?

Most of us have had these thoughts or daydreams, but have been quick to reality check ourselves that those dreams are too big, too unrealistic, or that they will probably never happen.

Reality check: You had it ALL wrong.

There is no such thing as a dream that is too big. There is no such thing as a goal that is impossible. Every woman that has accomplished anything great has surely had these thoughts run through her mind at some point...but she didn't listen.

I, myself, have had moments where I'm deep in a daydream of myself selling out the biggest theatres with women ready to hear me speak. I envision huge, sold out events where women travel internationally to be a part of what I've created. Have those thougts crept in and tried to make me doubt myself? ABSOLUTELY.

You shut that s* out.**

Thoughts dont have power unless we let them. That is why every time those doubts come into my brain as fear, I redirect that noise right back out. I replace them with inspiring thoughts, motivating encouragement, and remind myself that nothing is too out of reach.

Set yourself some big, scary goals.

What goals do you have for yourself? What goals do you have for your career, for your family, for yourself, and for your life? What are you striving to do, accomplish, and be? Make sure that you shove the idea out of your head that any goal is too big or too out of reach while you think of them.

A powerful woman sets goals and gets to work.

Set those goals. Remind yourself that you are a powerful woman. Get to work. These goals ain't gonna happen by themselves, girl. You're the one that's gonna make em' ALL happen.

Now, let's talk about those dreams.

When you talk about big dreams, it might make you (or those around you) uncomfortable. Dreams can be big, intimidating, and even daunting. It might feel like exactly what the name suggests...something that happens when you're asleep, but not in reality.

But dreams DO come true.

Dreams can absolutely become your reality. Do you think the most powerful, successful women out there ever told themselves, "Girl, those dreams are TOO big." HELL NO. They envisioned the things they wanted to do, and then started chasing after them.

Your dreams should be even bigger than your goals, because in reality, they go hand in hand. Goals and dreams are what make a woman get out of bed in the morning and get to work.

If you aren't working on your own, you're working on someone else's.

No matter what you do, you're working towards the goals and dreams of someone. They might as well be your own, right?

Start dreaming! Start creating goals! Make them things that make you feel alive, excited, and eager to make the damn thing happen! Because you, baby girl, absolutely can.

Powerful women know that nothing is out of their reach.

A woman determined to do great things is an unstoppable woman. When she sets her mind on something, she chases after in relentlessly. She knows she can. She knows she will. Nothing will stop her.

Get to work, girl.

Those dreams and goals aren't gonna make themselves happen. It's gonna be all because of YOU. A powerful woman with grit, aspirations, and visions of a life that is bigger, better, and well within her reach.

Set those goals big, and make those dreams even bigger. Tell yourself every morning when you take those first steps out of bed that this is your day to make that magic happen. Tell yourself that it's time to turn those dreams into your reality.

You are a powerful woman

8. She Jumps Despite Fear

THE KEY TO GROWTH IS
ACKNOWLEDGING YOUR
FEAR OF THE UNKNOWN
AND JUMPING IN
ANYWAY.

-Jen Sincero

She Jumps Despite Fear

Let's just call it like it is, shall we?

Fear is a little b**.**

It lingers in the background and pops up when you least expect it and when it is the least welcome. It's the guest that shows up to the party uninvited, and proceeds to overstay her welcome...every. single. time.

Fear has the ability to hold you back, make you uncomfortable, and drown you with anxiety. The result? Playing it safe, never going outside of your lane, and not doing things that are risky. But, that's not all.

Living in fear means not truly living.

Think about the things you've feared in life. Maybe it was death. Maybe it was losing a job. Maybe it was never meeting "the one." Maybe it was failing at something you really wanted to do well at.

So, you want to leave your job, start your own business, and be a six-figure entrepreneur. You daydream about being successful, traveling the world, and having a business that is absolutely booming. It's the millennial dream, right?

But something stops you from jumping all in.

What if you can't pay the bills? What if people think your business idea is stupid? What if nobody buys from you? What if your boyfriend or girlfriend thinks your idea is silly? What if it gets hard and you want to give up?

You're right. It was a silly idea anyways. Better to be safe than sorry. It was a crazy idea anyways...

Pause. Hold the f* up!**

That, ladies, is what we call fear taking over. That is fear filling your head with doubts, worries, and negativity. Telling you that your dreams are too big. Telling you that there's too many things that could go wrong. That is fear telling you to keep your feet on the ground.

What we need to do is JUMP.

Jump into the things that make you come alive. The things that light a spark inside of you. The things you are passionate about. The things you want to see, do, or be. Do not ever let fear hold you back from jumping into each and every one of these things.

Pushing past the fear takes power.

It's easy to listen to the fear and not try. It's much more simple to just stay complacent and not take the risks. But, does playing it safe really get you anywhere? Does it fill you up? Does it make you excited? Does it give you a life that you are proud and eager to talk about?

It takes a lot more work to choose to bust through the fear. To look it in the face and say, "I'm doing this, whether you like it or not." To listen to the doubts and the negativity fear is feeding us and say, "I'm more powerful than you."

Fear will always exist. It's how you handle it that changes the game.

I still have moments where the fear creeps back in. When I have a new project, a big event coming up, or something new and outside of my comfort zone, there are times where I can feel the fear try to linger.

The doubts, the anxiety, the worries...they all still exist. The difference is that I choose to not entertain them or give them any of my time or energy. I'm not here for it. I've decided fear has no place in my life anymore.

I've decided to always jump.

This is a rule I've chosen to live by as a powerful woman. The idea that anytime something stirs up the fear, it means I jump. I jump head first into the thing that scares me. I face it. I conquer it. I make it happen my way instead.

Jumping in takes faith in yourself, confidence in your choices, and knowing the power you have inside of you as a woman.

A powerful woman will never be stopped by fear.

She knows from life experience that big, incredible, amazing things happen outside of your comfort zone. Life-changing things happen. She knows that is where the fear lives, but she chooses to jump over and over again despite it.

Girl, get ready to JUMP.

There is nothing that can keep a powerful woman from doing whatever it is she wants to do in life, ESPECIALLY fear. The only way fear can stop her is if she lets it win. And she is not about to let that happen.

We are done letting fear call the shots. So, what will you jump into? Love? A new career path? Living life on your terms? Traveling? Setting boundaries? The opportunities are limitless and all yours to jump into.

You are a powerful woman

a. She Never Holds Herself Back

I DON'T BELIEVE IN
SORT OF HOLDING BACK,
YOU KNOW. LIFE ISN'T A
DRESS REHEARSAL!

-Kate Winslet

She Never Holds Herself Back

Living in a completely authentic manner can mean many different things. It can mean dancing to the beat of your own drum. It can mean living each day to its full potential. It can mean not holding yourself back from any one thing that you wish to do or be in life.

When I think of a woman that has held herself back, I think of someone who never gave herself permission. I think of a woman that didn't tell herself "YES" enough. I picture a woman that kept her voice small, her dreams hidden, and didn't just go for it when her heart was screaming at her to.

You don't get a redo at life.

Think about how much you would regret if you never gave yourself the green light in life. How many missed chances would you have? How many missed opportunities? How many regrets?

What would you miss out on?

Maybe you would miss out on finding the greatest love story ever. You might regret never applying for that dream job. Maybe you will look back and wish you would have done a lot of the things you wanted to do, but held yourself back from.

When I got sober, I vowed to make every single day of my life the best one that it could possibly be. I didn't want to look back and feel like I held myself back from anything in life anymore.

That meant not holding back in ANY area of my life.

That meant following my heart. That meant putting everything into making my desires my reality. Not holding back on one thing, no matter how big or small it was.

I gave myself permission. I took the trip. I announced the big, scary project. I believed that my huge, crazy dreams were possible. I told myself that I could (and would) make it all happen.

What do you need to say "YES" to?

What does a life well-lived look like to you?
Who is that woman? What does she look like?
How does she dress? How does she speak?
How does she live? What does she say "YES"
to?

There is no reason to not live life the way we
dream of living it. Even if it's not the way
someone else would live theirs, that doesn't
matter. This is your life and it's all about what
you want it to be.

Life your life the way you envision it.

It's easy to hold back in life when we think
about outside factors like the opinions or
judgement of others. It's easy to hold back in
life when we think about what everyone else is
doing. Stop watching! We spend too much time
watching and not enough time living.

Stop overthinking it and just LIVE.

For years I held myself back.

I didn't do the things I wanted to do because it wasn't the "normal" way to do it. Whether it was holding back my feelings in a relationship, staying in a job that I hated, or not speaking up when I didn't agree with something, I told myself that not ruffling feathers was the better way to live.

Clearly, that didn't f*ing last.**

As you can probably tell by now, I rewrote the HELL out of the narrative I had been telling myself for years. I realized how liberating it felt to give myself the green light and not look for it from other people. To tell myself "Girl, GO FOR IT" when it came to everything in my life.

There is power in living in a way where you feel like you are not holding back at anything. There is pride in knowing that you followed your heart in every way. There is no regret. No wishing you'd done it differently. No disappointment in not at least trying.

Live your truth and live it loudly.

How amazing will it feel one day to look back and know that you have lived your life exactly the way you wanted to? To know that you never kept any of yourself quiet or small. To know that you went all in.

A powerful woman never holds herself back in life.

She knows the value of telling herself "YES." She gives herself the green light instead of looking for it from someone else. She gives herself permission to do, be, and live exactly as she desires.

A powerful woman is real, authentic, and purposeful in her life. She doesn't care if people don't agree with it. She doesn't bother herself with conforming. She lives...and she lives life full throttle, full steam ahead. Never holding herself back from any little thing.

You are a powerful woman

10. She Empowers Other Women

NOTHING CAN DISTURB THE PEACE OF AN EMPOWERED WOMAN. NO SMALL VOICE, NO IGNORANT OPINION CAN RATTLE THE STRENGTH OF A WOMAN WHO HAS ALREADY DECIDED THAT SHE IS ENOUGH.

-Cara Alwill Leyba

She Empowers Other Women

We see this one posted and blogged about so much on social media that surely it must be the norm already, right? We all are going out of our way to raise up other women and cheer them on, right ladies!?

I have a strong feeling that if you are reading this book you are at least somewhat already on board with this idea. But in case you're not 100% on that train yet, let's chat about it!

There is room for all of us at the top.

A powerful woman knows that there is room for all of us to succeed. There is more than enough money, enough success, and enough fame to go around. She knows that all of us can rise to the top of our game without holding others back.

Jealousy, cattiness, and nastiness need not exist in a powerful woman's world. EVER.

Raise up the women around you.

There should be a mutual respect among women with power that are doing their thing. They see other women working hard and encourage them. They see other women accomplishing things and clap for them.

It's NOT about competition.

There is space in the world for every single woman to do what she does, and to do it well. It's not about who is the best. It's not about who makes more money. It's not about how many followers they have. It's about changing the world together as women.

It's about rewriting the narrative of success. It's about knowing that we can all be the best at what we do. It's about showing the world together that women can do anything they set their sights on.

It's about making a statement together that we are a force to be reckoned with...whether it's in our accomplishments, our earnings, our lifestyle, or our rights.

Women are stronger in numbers.

There is something about a group of women empowering one another that just oozes high vibes. You can see the positive energy and strength that radiates from a group of women coming together over something they are passionate about.

No being catty, jealous, or vindictive.

A powerful woman? She would never waste her time on such things! She walks away from situations and people that drag in those negative vibes.

She has no time for women being catty. She has no space in her world for jealousy. She does not allow negativite or malicious people's energy into her own world.

She is all about that positivity.

You have the power and the right to decide what type of women you let into your life and into your circle.

Practice what you preach, girl!

Bring in the women that support you, but make sure you are doing the same. How are you empowering the women around you? How are you raising them up? How are you supporting your fellow sisters in the world?

There's a revolution starting, and it's full of women.

I have really dove into the world of connecting with, supporting, and collaborating with other women in recent years. It's been a total game changer!

I can genuinely say that I had no idea just how many women there were out there that were ready and willing to support me.
It has been so beautiful and refreshing to collaborate with women (both locally and online) and support each other. It's exactly what inspired me to start hosting my own live events.

I suddenly saw all of these women ready and LOOKING for other women to empower and grow with.

A powerful women empowers the women around her.

She doesn't just work with her head down. She doesn't focus on her success only. She is constantly looking for opportunities to connect, encourage, empower, and grow WITH the women around her, not against them.

She never feels jealous towards other women. She never speaks to them in ways that are catty, rude, or condescending. She does not feel threatened by another woman's success. She sees the women around her as her equals.

She sees the power we have as women.

There is so much opportunity for the empowered women of today. There are big things happening for the powerful women of today. Not just for one of us, for ALL of us.

It's time ladies. Grab your girls. Raise them up. We're about to change the world...TOGETHER.

You are a powerful woman

11 She's Not Afraid to Ruffle A Few Feathers

YOU CAN BE THE
RIPEST, JUICIEST PEACH
IN THE WORLD
AND THERE'S STILL
GOING TO BE SOMEBODY
WHO HATES PEACHES.

-Dita
Von Teese

She's Not Afraid To Ruffle A Few Feathers

There is always going to be someone that doesn't like you. Not everyone will be your biggest fan. You can live your life like a saint and someone is still going to have a problem with it, so you might as well do whatever the f*** you want, right?

Don't be afraid to do it YOUR way.

Women today are breaking through norms and judgements like its their jobs. Women have began to realize that living your life the way you want to is bound to ruffle some feathers along the way, and thats okay.

We can't make everyone happy, and honestly, why should we?

Ruffling a few feathers, dancing to the beat of your own drum, living life on YOUR terms, and shaking things up a bit is NOT a bad thing. It's a good thing. It's a powerful thing.

Take the opinions of others lightly.

Not every opinion, judgment, or criticism you receive as a woman will be negative, but some will be. And, guess what? People are more than allowed to have them and voice them. What's crucial is that you realize that you don't have to do a damn thing with them or about them.

Take what you need and leave the rest.

Take away the knowledge and the growth you can from what others say or feel about something. Take the good, learn from it, grow from it, but DEFINITELY leave the bad.

We, as women, sometimes have a tendency to take on the negative words, opinions, and judgements of others. We might internalize them and take on their negative energy. We might believe what others say about us and let it dictate how we live and exist moving forward.

You are NOT what others say about you.

Let's be honest...there are some mean girls out there. Odds are that you've encountered them a few times along the way. There are women out there that might not want to see you succeed. Those aren't your women.

If you've ever been criticized or attacked wrongly by another woman for how you live your life, you know how nasty it can feel. It raises the question immediately of, "Why can't we all just play nice?" For some women, they sadly might never get there.

The only opinion that matters is your own.

I'll be honest, I know there are probably some women out there that can't stand me. They probably think I'm too open. I'm too much. I'm too out there. They probably talk s*** about my photos, my posts, and my vibe as a whole.

And, trust me, when you swear a lot on the internet someone is ALWAYS going to be in your DMs about how "unladylike" you are.

I have received a lot of hate for doing things my way. Messages telling me that I'm wrong. Comments criticizing the content I create. I've even been sent things on accident meant to be talking about me behind my back.
#FAIL girl.

Guess what? They don't stop me.

I know that I'm going to ruffle a few feathers. People ain't gonna like me. I know I'm going to shake things up a bit. I'm allowed to. I'm not afraid to. And that...that is powerful as f***.

It's time to not give a f*.**

There is a quote that has floated around for years and been used by many people about a lion not concerning itself with the opinion of sheep. It's a bit harsh, but insanely accurate when talking about this topic.

People that choose to be negative, criticize, or belittle are so below the powerful women they attack. They truly are sheep among lions.

A powerful woman ruffles feathers gladly.

She knows she can live life her way. She knows she can do things differently. She knows how much power there is in not being defined by what others think about her. She knows she doesn't have to conform.

The more we choose to break the norm and challenge how others see women today, the more powerful we become.

It's time we ruffle those feathers and get those panties in a twist.

The powerful women of today didn't get to where they are by playing it safe. They got there because they weren't afraid to do life on their own terms.

They weren't afraid to push the envelope. They weren't afraid to disrupt the norm. They weren't afraid to take their power and use the f*** out of it.

You are a powerful woman

12. She Knows She Is Unstoppable

NOBODY GETS TO TELL
YOU HOW BIG YOUR
DREAMS CAN BE.

-Rachel Hollis

She Knows She Is Unstoppable

Women are f***ing UNSTOPPABLE in today's world. Just look at how far we've come! Look at how much we've progressed and made change for ourselves over time. From having little to no rights to running for president, girl, we've made some major moves.

What's really made this type of revolution happen is realizing that we cannot be stopped. We cannot be silenced. We cannot be held back. We cannot be told that we can't do any less than any of our male counterparts.

Who run the world? GIRLS.

But this idea of being unstoppable doesn't only apply to the ones standing with a microphone. It doesn't only apply to the women marching on Washington for Women's Rights. It isn't only for the women making six-figures...it applies to YOU. It applies to ME. It applies to ALL of us.

We all have the power.

There is no privilege, no silver spoon, no welcome key to the city given to these women in the spotlight. Nobody gave them the power to do what they are doing. They knew they had the power and they ran with it.

YOU have the power to be unstoppable in YOU.

Even if you haven't uncovered it yet, each and every one of us has the power to do big things. We all have the ability to chase after what we are passionate about. We all have the power to change the world not just for women, but for EVERYONE.

Women are changing the game. They are realizing how unstoppable they truly are and running with it.

It's a POWERFUL time to be a woman.

We are doing more, being more, and leaving our mark more than ever before. It's one hell of a time to be a woman.

Realizing what you are capable of is a huge, life-shifting, awakening moment as a woman. Realizing that you have unlimited, never-ending potential to do ANYTHING you want to do...now, THAT'S BIG.

Watch how your life will shift.

In my own journey, once I realized my potential and the power I had within me to do anything I wanted to, my life changed forever. I realized that I, too, was truly unstoppable.

My business blew up. I was designing my life every day to be one that I loved living. I was taking bigger risks. I was following my heart. I was chasing after what lit me up inside. I was THRIVING.

Realize the power you have within you.

If you haven't mastered this one yet, get to work on it, sister. Do the work. Get through the bulls*** and knock out the limiting beliefs. Drill it into that pretty little head of yours that you have all the power you need within you. You can't be stopped.

It's been inside you all along.

The power we have as women isn't something that just shows up one day on its own. It has been inside of each and every one of us since we were little girls. We just didn't realize it until we started looking for it.

It's time to find it, girl! Get on board with this train of women that know and believe that they are unstoppable.

I know you've been watching us. It's time to join us!

We're building this army of women that will not back down. This incredible community that is influencing millions of people and inspiring them every single day.

We want YOU to be a part of this movement. We want YOU standing tall right next to us. Put your lipstick on, get in those heels, and join the ranks, girl!

The movement is NOW.

If you're reading this, then you are already a part of it. You have realized that deep inside of you, you have something more. You have something bigger inside of you that is meant to shine.

A powerful woman will NOT be stopped.

She knows her potential and she knows her power. She harnesses it and uses it to make a difference in her world and the world of all women.

We are f*ing UNSTOPPABLE.**

There is nobody that can tell us "NO." There is nobody that can tell us to sit down. There is no one that can tell us to be quiet. Unless we allow them to stop us. And we already know, that these women CANNOT be stopped.

You are a powerful woman

Mantras For A Powerful Woman

- I am unstoppable.
- My dreams are within my reach.
- I can achieve big, crazy things.
- I am in my control of my life.
- I am thriving.
- Today is MY day.
- I am open to the blessing coming my way.
- I choose to be happy.
- I am worthy of love.
- I am ENOUGH.
- I am living the life of my dreams.
- I choose things that feel good.
- I am vibrating light & love.
- Money is always available to me.
- I am open to receiving abundance.
- I have the strength to overcome ANY challenge.
- I follow my heart.
- I am a powerful woman.

Powerful Woman Manifesto

Today I choose to be powerful.

I choose to love myself first & fearlessly. I will love & accept every inch of my physical self. I will honor the woman that I am.

I will not allow disrespect into my space. I will follow my heart in everything that I choose to do (with my head close behind). I will stand solid in my own opinions & beliefs. My voice will not be silenced. I will be heard. I will empower the women around me to use their voice & their power.

I will chase after my goals. I will work towards my even bigger dreams. I will jump, despite fear. I choose to never hold myself back in any way.

I am not afraid to ruffle a few feathers. I am not afraid to live on my own terms. I know that I am unstoppable. I am strong. I am beautiful.

I am a woman...a damn POWERFUL one.

About The Author

As an entrepreneur, makeup artist, self-published author, YouTuber, mindset coach, podcast host, live event host and blogger, Sarah Ordo is your not-so-average Millennial craving to leave her mark on this world in more ways than one.

Sarah's award-winning on location hair and makeup company (based out of Detroit), 24Luxe Hair & Makeup, has been styling women for their special events since 2013. Her social media pages reach thousands of followers daily featuring a variety of beauty, health, lifestyle, sobriety, and wellness posts. Her YouTube videos documenting and following her sobriety have reached millions of viewers internationally, and have even been featured on Dateline NBC. Sarah has been featured on and interviewed for numerous media outlets including MTV, NBC, and Inspiring Lives Magazine.

On her podcast Her Best F***ing Life, Sarah loves to talk about all topics surrounding how to create a life you love, your best life possible. The episodes feature a no-bullsh*t approach to life, amazing guest interviews, and a whole lot of swearing. On her website, sarahordo.com, Sarah blogs about living sober, self-love, mental health, and many other raw, honest topics. She also sells merchandise on her website for her books and podcast.

Sarah also hosts live female empowerment events in the Detroit area. Her infamous Her Best F***ing Brunch events draw in women from all areas.

Sober as F*** was the first full-length memoir and book written by Sarah, released in May 2017. She has gone on to publish numerous other books which are all available on Amazon & Kindle.

Connect with Sarah:
www.sarahordo.com
Youtube: Sarah Ordo
Instagram: @24Luxe_Sarah
Podcast: Her Best F***ing Life (on iTunes & Stitcher)
Books: Amazon & Kindle

Made in the USA
Las Vegas, NV
12 March 2022

45501412R00074